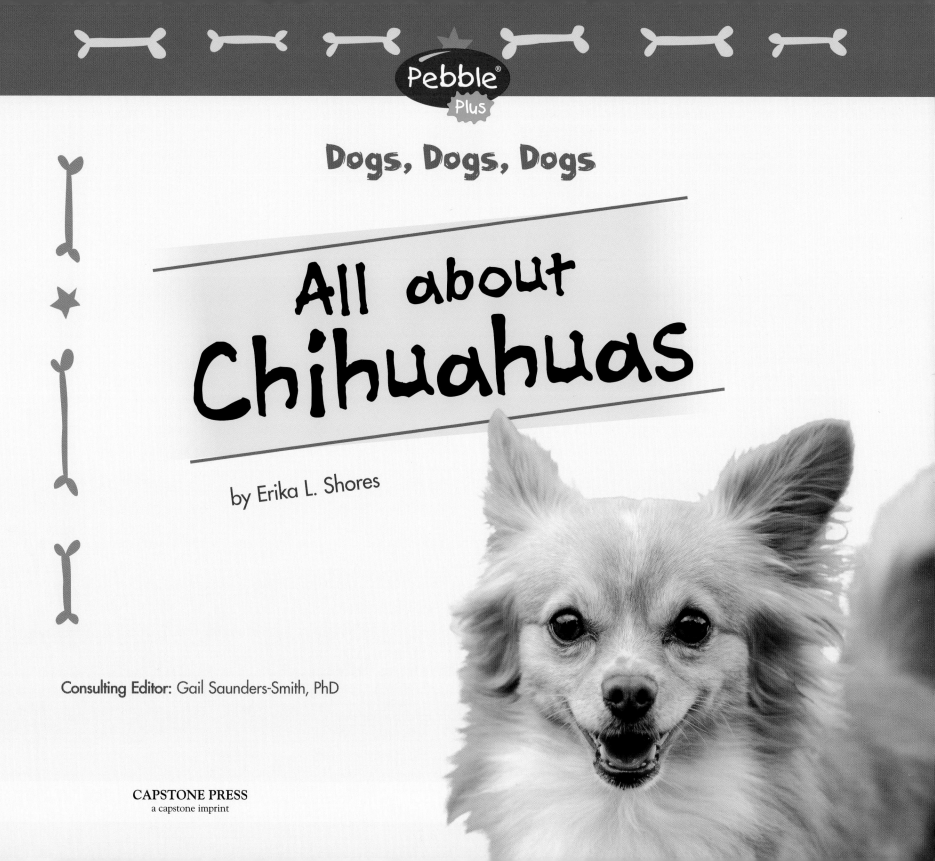

Pebble® Plus

Dogs, Dogs, Dogs

All about Chihuahuas

by Erika L. Shores

Consulting Editor: Gail Saunders-Smith, PhD

CAPSTONE PRESS
a capstone imprint

Pebble Plus is published by Capstone Press,
1710 Roe Crest Drive, North Mankato, Minnesota 56003.
www.capstonepub.com

Library of Congress Cataloging-in-Publication Data
Shores, Erika L., 1976–
All about chihuahuas / by Erika L. Shores.
p. cm.—(Pebble plus. dogs, dogs, dogs)
Includes bibliographical references and index.
Summary: "Full-color photographs and simple text provide a brief introduction to Chihuahuas"—Provided by publisher.
ISBN 978-1-4296-8724-9 (library binding)
ISBN 978-1-62065-292-3 (ebook PDF)
1. Chihuahua (Dog breed)—Juvenile literature. I. Title.
SF429.C45S56 2013
636.76—dc23   2011049818

Editorial Credits
Juliette Peters, designer; Marcie Spence, media researcher; Kathy McColley, production specialist

Photo Credits
Capstone Studio: Karon Dubke, 15, 19; iStockphoto: DPLight, 17, JodiJacobson, 13; Shutterstock: Aaron Amat, 9,
AnetaPics, 1, DRogatnev, 3, Gertjan Hooijer, 21, gillmar, 7, Jiri Vaclavek, cover, Lisa F. Young, 5, Nikolai Pozdeev, 11

Note to Parents and Teachers

The Dogs, Dogs, Dogs series supports national science standards related to life science. This
book describes and illustrates Chihuahuas. The images support early readers in understanding
the text. The repetition of words and phrases helps early readers learn new words. This book
also introduces early readers to subject-specific vocabulary words, which are defined in the
Glossary section. Early readers may need assistance to read some words and to use the Table of
Contents, Glossary, Read More, Internet Sites, and Index sections of the book.

Printed in the United States of America in North Mankato, Minnesota.
042012   006682CGF12

Table of Contents

Tiny Dogs

Chihuahuas are the world's smallest breed of dog. They weigh only 2 to 6 pounds (1 to 3 kilograms).

Chihuahuas may be small,

but they have a spunky temperament.

A dog's behavior and personality

make up its temperament.

The Chihuahua Look

Big eyes and perky ears give

Chihuahuas an alert look.

Their eyes and ears tune in

to everything they see and hear.

Chihuahuas have long

or short coats.

Chihuahuas can be brown,

black, white, cream, or tan.

They can also be a mix of colors.

Puppy Time

Female Chihuahuas give birth
to three to six puppies.
Puppies grow quickly. They are
adults after 6 to 18 months.
Chihuahuas live 12 to 15 years.

Doggie Duties

Chihuahuas belong to a group of dogs called toy breeds. But they aren't toys. Owners must watch small dogs closely. Little dogs can get hurt jumping from high places.

Chihuahuas should be well-behaved.

Owners take their dogs to classes

to teach them to sit, stay, and come.

Learning these commands is called

obedience training.

Owners should brush Chihuahuas

once or twice a week.

Oils in Chihuahuas' coats help

keep their fur clean.

They rarely need baths.

Perky Pets

Fun and playful Chihuahuas make great pets. Owners love their smart and sassy dogs.

Glossary

alert—watchful and ready to act

breed—a certain kind of animal within an animal group

coat—an animal's hair or fur

command—an order to do something

obedience—following rules and commands

sassy—bold and lively

spunky—full of courage

temperament—the combination of a dog's personality and behavior

Read More

Green, Sara. *Chihuahuas.* Dog Breeds. Minneapolis: Bellwether Media, 2010.

Hengel, Katherine. *Chipper Chihuahuas.* Dog Daze. Edina, Minn.: ABDO Pub., 2011.

Lunis, Natalie. *Chihuahua: Señor Tiny.* Little Dogs Rock! New York: Bearport Pub., 2009.

Internet Sites

FactHound offers a safe, fun way to find Internet sites related to this book. All of the sites on FactHound have been researched by our staff.

Here's all you do:

Visit *www.facthound.com*

Type in this code: 9781429687249

 Check out projects, games and lots more at
www.capstonekids.com

Index

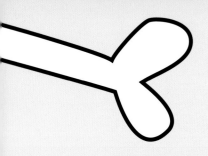

Word Count: 199
Grade: 1
Early-Intervention Level: 16